The TWELVE DAYS of CHRISTMAS

A Christmas Carol

Illustrated by
MIKE EAGLE

A GOLDEN BOOK • NEW YORK

Western Publishing Company, Inc., Racine, Wisconsin 53404

On the first day of Christmas
My true love gave to me
A partridge in a pear tree.

On the second day of Christmas
My true love gave to me
Two turtledoves
And a partridge in a pear tree.

On the third day of Christmas
My true love gave to me
Three French hens,
Two turtledoves,
And a partridge in a pear tree.

On the fourth day of Christmas
My true love gave to me
Four calling birds,

Three French hens,
Two turtledoves,
And a partridge in a pear tree.

On the fifth day of Christmas
My true love gave to me
Five gold rings,

Four calling birds,
Three French hens,
Two turtledoves,
And a partridge in a pear tree.

On the sixth day of Christmas
My true love gave to me
Six geese a-laying,

Five gold rings,
Four calling birds,
Three French hens,
Two turtledoves,
And a partridge in a pear tree.

On the seventh day of Christmas
My true love gave to me
Seven swans a-swimming,

Six geese a-laying,
Five gold rings,
Four calling birds,
Three French hens,
Two turtledoves,
And a partridge in a pear tree.

On the eighth day of Christmas
My true love gave to me
Eight maids a-milking,

Seven swans a-swimming,
Six geese a-laying,
Five gold rings,
Four calling birds,
Three French hens,
Two turtledoves,
And a partridge in a pear tree.

On the ninth day of Christmas
My true love gave to me
Nine ladies waiting,

Eight maids a-milking,
Seven swans a-swimming,
Six geese a-laying,
Five gold rings,
Four calling birds,
Three French hens,
Two turtledoves,
And a partridge in a pear tree.

On the tenth day of Christmas
My true love gave to me
Ten lords a-leaping,

Nine ladies waiting,
Eight maids a-milking,
Seven swans a-swimming,
Six geese a-laying,
Five gold rings,
Four calling birds,
Three French hens,
Two turtledoves,
And a partridge in a pear tree.

On the eleventh day of Christmas
My true love gave to me
Eleven pipers piping,

Ten lords a-leaping,
Nine ladies waiting,
Eight maids a-milking,
Seven swans a-swimming,
Six geese a-laying,

Five gold rings,
Four calling birds,
Three French hens,
Two turtledoves,
And a partridge in a pear tree.

On the twelfth day of Christmas
My true love gave to me
Twelve drummers drumming,
Eleven pipers piping,
Ten lords a-leaping,
Nine ladies waiting,
Eight maids a-milking,

Seven swans a-swimming,
Six geese a-laying,
Five gold rings,
Four calling birds,
Three French hens,
Two turtledoves,

And a partridge in a pear tree.